curious about
TEAM ROPING
BY RACHEL GRACK
AMICUS LEARNING
AF270026

What are you

curious about?

CHAPTER THREE

Bringing Home the Win
PAGE **18**

Curious About is published by
Amicus Learning, an imprint of Amicus
P.O. Box 227, Mankato, MN 56002
www.amicuspublishing.us

Editors: Megan Siewert and Ana Brauer
Series Designer: Kathleen Petelinsek
Book Designer and Photo Researcher: Kathleen Petelinsek

Library of Congress Cataloging-in-Publication Data
Names: Koestler-Grack, Rachel A., 1973– author.
Title: Curious about team roping / by Rachel Grack.
Description: Mankato, MN : Curious About is published by
Amicus Learning, [2025] | Series: Curious about Rodeo |
Includes bibliographical references and index. | Audience: Ages
6–9 years | Audience: Grades 2–3 | Summary: "Learn how
cowboys and cowgirls (and their horses) compete in team roping
rodeo events in this question-and-answer book for elementary-
aged readers. Includes infographics and back matter to support
research skills along with table of contents, glossary, books and
websites for further research, and index"—Provided by publisher.
Identifiers: LCCN 2024015017 (print) |
LCCN 2024015018 (ebook) |
ISBN 9798892000895 (lib bdg) |
ISBN 9798892001472 (paperback) |
ISBN 9798892002059 (ebook)
Subjects: LCSH: Team roping—Juvenile literature.
Classification: LCC GV1834.45.T42 K64
2025 (print) | LCC GV1834.45.T42 (ebook) |
DDC 791.8/4—dc23/eng/20240507
LC record available at https://lccn.loc.gov/2024015017
LC ebook record available at https://lccn.loc.gov/2024015018

Photo Credits: Alamy Stock Photo/Luc Novovitch, 13, 19
(second from bottom, right), Xinhua, cover, 1; Dreamstime/
Derrick Neill, 2 (left), 8–9, Pierre Jean Durieu, 10–11,
19 (middle); Shutterstock/Jackson Stock Photography, 2
(right), 7, 17, 14–15, 19, Macrovector, 16, 22, 23, mark
reinstein, 5, YES Market Media, 3, 20–21, Yeti studio, 6

Printed in China

What is team roping?

It is a timed rodeo sport. A two-person team on horseback tries to rope a running **steer**. The header ropes it around its head or horns. The heeler catches its hind legs. Got it! The fastest time wins.

DID YOU KNOW?
Team roping is the only professional rodeo sport where cowboys and cowgirls compete against each other in the same event.

In team roping, ropers work together to catch the steer.
Heeler
Header
THROWING ROPES

Is roping hard?

Very! Learning to rope takes practice. Timing a throw is tricky, especially on horseback. Ropers do not have time to think about riding or directing their horses. Instead, ropers work with their horses every day. They have excellent **horsemanship**. They train their horses to follow running patterns and body cues.

Ropers have to
time their throws
perfectly or they
might miss the steer.

Which horses are best for team roping?
TEAM ROPING GEAR
Western saddle provides a safer ride
Splint boots protect hooves and legs
Horn wraps protect the steer from breaks and rope burns

Most ropers use American quarter horses. They can be trained for either job. The horses have both speed and power. They are fast right at the start. They charge out of the box. Heeling horses can make quick turns and sudden stops. Heading horses use their powerful build to handle and hold the steer.

The riders, horses, and steer all wear special gear to protect them during the event.

What happens first?

DID YOU KNOW?
Roper boxes are on either side of the chute. The header backs his horse into the box on left side. The heeler takes the right.

Chute

Both ropers wait in a box. The steer is released from the **chute**. It gets a head start. It breaks through the **barrier rope**. Then, the header takes off into the arena. The heeler follows and **hazes** the steer. Headers throw the first rope. He must make a fair catch to continue.

The ropers must give the steer a head start, otherwise they break the barrier.

When does the heeler throw?

The heeler throws after the header makes a fair catch. He needs to rope both hind legs. The header turns the steer by its head, so its back legs face the heeler. Now, it's the heeler's turn to throw. He catches both feet. He quickly wraps the rope around the **saddle horn**.

DID YOU KNOW?
The act of wrapping the rope around the saddle horn is called the dally.

The heeler can't make his throw until after the header finishes turning the steer.
CACTUS
THE EVENT

DID YOU KNOW?

Headers and heelers use different kinds of ropes. Heeler ropes are stiffer to help catch the steer's legs. Header ropes are softer and shorter.

When does the clock stop?

Two more steps to go! First, the ropers must stretch the steer. They back up their horses to pull the **slack** from the ropes. This stretches out the steer's legs. Next, they turn their horses to face each other. The clock stops.

Does the steer get hurt?

It might. Good ropers never hurt steers on purpose. But there is always a chance something could go wrong. Rodeos have rules to keep animals safe and healthy. Contestants who break these rules get fined. Many rodeos have on-site vets in case of accidents.

FAIR CATCHES

Clean Horn Catch:
around both horns

Half-Head Catch:
around neck and one horn

Neck Catch:
around the neck

Steers often wear horn wraps for extra padding.

Are there rules?

Absolutely! Headers cannot break the barrier too soon. This adds 10 seconds to the team's time. Both ropers need clean catches. Teams get disqualified if the header fails to make a fair catch. There is a 5-second **penalty** if the heeler only ropes one leg. Every second counts!

1
GATE OF THE CHUTE OPENS:
CLOCK STARTS

2
STEER RUNS INTO THE ARENA:
NECK ROPE PULLS TIGHT AND BREAKS AWAY

3
BARRIER ROPE DROPS:
ROPERS BURST OUT OF THE BOX

4
HEADER MAKES A FAIR CATCH:
HEELER ROPES BOTH LEGS

5
ROPERS PULL THE SLACK AND FACE EACH OTHER:
CLOCK STOPS

What's a winning time?

Team ropers have
a chance to win a
large money prize.

Most professional ropers finish in under 10 seconds. Top ropers do it even faster. Winning times are often tenths of a second apart. The world record is 3.3 seconds! That time will be hard to beat. Grab a rope and start practicing!

ASK MORE QUESTIONS

Where can I learn to rope?

Can you get rich roping?

Try a BIG QUESTION: Could I ride and rope at the same time?

SEARCH FOR ANSWERS

Search the library catalog or the Internet.
A librarian, teacher, or parent can help you.

Using Keywords
Find the looking glass.

Keywords are the most important words in your question.

If you want to know:

- about roping classes near you, type: YOUTH ROPING [YOUR CITY/STATE]

- about team roping prizes, type: TEAM ROPING WINNINGS

FIND GOOD SOURCES

Here are some good, safe sources you can use in your research.
Your librarian can help you find more.

Books

Tie-Down Roping
by Rachel Grack, 2025.

Calf Roping
by Rochelle Groskreutz, 2021.

Internet Sites

Britannica: Team Roping
https://www.britannica.com/sports/team-roping
Britannica is an encyclopedia with educational information on many topics. Learn more about rodeos and team roping.

Kiddle: Rodeo Facts for Kids
https://kids.kiddle.co/Rodeo
Kiddle is an online encyclopedia for kids. Search for information on a wide variety of educational topics.

Every effort has been made to ensure that these websites are appropriate for children. However, because of the nature of the Internet, it is impossible to guarantee that these sites will remain active indefinitely or that their contents will not be altered.

SHARE AND TAKE ACTION

Watch team roping.
Ask an adult to help you find videos of team roping events.

Take horseback riding classes.
You need to learn to ride before you rope!

Rope a dummy.
Sign up for a roping class near you!

About the Author

Rachel Grack has been writing children's nonfiction for twenty-five years. She lives on a ranch in the heart of rodeo country (southern Arizona). Some evenings, she wanders over to watch her neighbors in friendly roping competitions. A western restaurant in town offers weekly bull riding and mutton busting. But Rachel much prefers a quiet ride on her gentle paint horse, Lady.